D1571096

never to be titled

this collection was never meant to be titled.

<u>dedication:</u>

for those who believe they are monsters,
are not getting better,
or feel daunted by the journey.

<u>to those who encouraged me</u>
<u>to be a sellout</u>

they cried,
voices blaring louder than a siren,
"name your collection or build a
guillotine!"
and so, i stuck out my neck,
grinned, and said, "i have always wondered
what it was like to be in my head less."

"—i find it only fair that i introduce myself in the only way that i know how. this is my office. you're welcome inside. it's a place where i cannot lie to myself, and i won't lie to you."

                                        – unheard words

table of contents

<u>before we begin:</u>

to those reading who do not know me,
you will see fragmented poems
thrust in what seems to be a chaotic
washing machine and churned out.
i have thought about organizing them
a thousand times but finally settled
that no thoughts are stagnant,
and mine certainly are not categorized.
so, what could possibly be more
authentic— more realistic—
than poems in no particular order. . .

brink of extinction

come the last of your kind—
extinct creature on the edge of time
where life did little to preserve you
in its minutes and moments
the writer of words— of worlds
a legend in ink and myth of mind
for there no longer exists
what was once commonly called
"a poet"

<u>lesson from the general</u>

the lifeblood of our existence is love.
it is what gives us purpose—
what gives us hope.
but it is also the most
wildly dangerous emotion.
for what war was not waged
in the pretense of love?

<u>awaiting new lectures</u>

they said,
"don't make a mountain out of a molehill,"
but they have neglected to teach me how
to make a molehill out of a mountain.

tree before the seed

oh, darling but do you not see?
i was the giving tree,
and i entrusted you with a seed
      that you did not plant
because you never wanted me.

<u>make the oxygen a home</u>

breathe, the shadows whisper
as if to warn me
that the darkness feeds on CO_2.
i wonder when they started
to recognize me as their own.

<u>a broken soliloquy</u>

in the midst of the darkness
will we ever find the light?
will we see the dawn of day,
or is it time to say goodnight?

<u>weaponize the words</u>

fork-tongued girl
who speaks with venom,
how did you make
intelligence lethal?

<u>years of summer sunsets</u>

forget-me-nots
and butterscotch
through our summer days
then gone in a haze
of the ocean breeze
and sun rays.

<u>walt</u>

words murmured through eons
long ago, remembered by the wind,
swept through seasons of life and decay
and they say,
"resist much
obey little."
the grass whispers as it waves
through tomorrows and todays.

twisted perception

i am the monster under your bed,
and i have a truth to tell too.
we are not here to hurt or harm
my duty was always to protect you.

<u>healing away the talons and claws</u>

there are whisper words stuck in my head,
spinning through my thoughts
like an unhinged ferris wheel,
and they murmur the same words
in a morbid ritual,
"it is not your fault you became a monster,
but it is your fault that you stayed one."

<u>mirror, mirror</u>

we will continue to strive
to protect ourselves from the demons.
but somewhere in the journey
our efforts transform us
into them,
and we find ourselves
stuck in a mirror—
blocking ourselves
from healing.

<u>a funeral for innocence</u>

the children are singing their silly song
but each one is a dirge,
and we light the pyres at dawn
while you escape the grip of the world.

<u>even the stars remain ignorant</u>

what would come of us
if we sought a peace treaty
within ourselves?
would we find that we,
ourselves,
have settled down next to
our mental illnesses
and have conversations
that the universe itself
could learn from?

glass castle, broken crown

fill my heart with glass then break it
step on it and smash the pieces
into my arteries— into my veins
and anytime i look at someone with love
i will feel a grinding in my chest
every pulse as painful
as dragging a last breath
and i will rethink you again

<u>color the uncolored</u>

so, we give and give and give ourselves
until only an outline remains...
and i have never been one to enjoy
uncolored coloring books.

conforming to the naughty list

forgiveness is not an extensive element in
our world—
a rare gem we are quick to gift away.
no matter how much we find,
we may hold it until
we feel the time is right
to give to someone else,
but rarely is that present
ever addressed to ourselves—
vying for coal within our stockings.

<u>do not stay progress</u>

i was once told,
"there exist three types of people
the breaker, the broken, and the breaking."
but that statement cannot be true.
for i believe there are four:
the healer, the healed, and the healing,
and what is the fourth you may ask?
well, it is the hesitant. . .
the ones unsure if they deserve healing
at all.

a testimony of my eyes

peace is gentle.
peace is kind.
and peace is very hard to find,
but what it is not
is imaginary.

<u>mother, oh mother, please do not frown</u>

we are born from nothing—
birthed from darkness into light,
and so, we know darkness
intimately.
but the darkness fears we will
forget it as our mother,
so it tacks us with shadows
to follow and remind us
we are beings of the dark.

<u>matte black</u>

"if a color were named
after you, what would it be?"
"black that is matte
with no shine," you answered.
"yes, matte black would be dark,
but it would be mine."

singing songs in strait jackets

oh, the terror— the horror
to be out of your mind,
and out of your head,
but to conform— to be normal
would be torturous instead.

<u>wedding at the mansion</u>

"until death do us part,"
fear vowed, flicking a snake-tongue.
but you solemnly shook your head.
"i have never been one for toxic love."

to the rocks that can listen

remember that otters
choose a favorite stone
and they stick it in their pouch
and choose no other
despite that others are more shiny
less corroded
unscarred and unused
but that otter wishes for comfort
to know the edges and the dips
so choose an otter
who chooses you

<u>do we follow the nursery rhymes?</u>

you know soldiers do not surrender.
so, stand.
take your weary feet and pick them up.
they will lead you to the land
of milk and honey—
or somewhere else entirely.

<u>unbreakables</u>

in the wake of destruction,
we will awaken,
rise,
and find peace.

<u>untitled</u>

the silhouette and echo
loved to dance and play,
but when all the light and sound died
they began to fade away.

<u>sidewalk summers</u>

when we were younger
we carved our names in cement
so we would be side-by-side
and they would never forget
but i wonder if we would have
done what we did
if we were wise enough to realize
we would change from those kids

to the true owners

path-walker, forest-dweller
step onto the gravel
rocks digging into your soles
and in the midst of the city
redress and don your headdress
for you once owned this land
before claimed by the white man
who knew little of the earth
your ancestors call to you
place your hands upon the bark
of the dwindling trees
they have not eradicated you yet

<u>describe me in truth</u>
<u>and i will still stand</u>

so maybe i am emotionless—
a cold, stone-hearted bitch,
but at least ice and rock
will never need a stitch.

<u>to shatter in silence</u>

"if a tree falls in a forest
and no one is around to hear it
does it make a sound?" they asked.
but do humans make a sound
when they break?
if they do not,
do they remain unbroken?

<u>drowning the lilies</u>

perhaps it is ourselves
that dictate the pain in our lives.
if life offers us fear
and we are already afraid
then we have amplified our problem,
for watering lilies
at the beginning of a rainstorm
merely drowns them faster.

<u>rebel's revolutionary lullaby</u>

our humanity cannot be
ripped from our soul.
they may break our bones
and peal away our skin,
but who we are remains intact
if we decide we want to.
there is no power to silence a spirit.
it is us who break ourselves, and it often
comes in the form of apathy and hatred.

<u>bird song</u>

chatter birds chatter
then scatter all scared
always afraid of the unknown
of what could be there—

farmer's query

a farmer petitioned congress
with a query to be read,
attempting to find an answer in chaos,
and this is what it said,
"i have too many pigs," he wrote.
"and all must be slaughtered,
but they squeal and struggle too much—
escape and then they scatter.
i need to know how to handle this—
with the pigs inside my pen,
for i have lost their complacency.
how do i soothe and quell them?"
the politician wrote back that next day
"it seems, dear farmer, the pigs coup.
so, gather them in the pen outside,
and, if you can, get your hands on
a show pig or two.
lead the shows into the slaughterhouse
so the others can see their behavior,
and once your pigs see the prizes quiet
they will not fuss nor bother.
then when you have completed that
quietly lead the show pigs out the door.
the fattened hogs will not see it coming
when you lead them to the bloodied floor."

greek myth sans pandora

hope seems to be theseus
in every labyrinth.
it is sent out into the world
not meant to survive,
and each time it emerges
there is a higher will to kill it.

<u>a question of home</u>

if home is where the heart is
why have you not found it within
your chest?

a healing note

music heals us in ways that no salve could.
there exists no greater remedy
for the pain within the mansion
than that of the gentle relation,
or violent retaliation,
in the form of notes and melodies.
i believe it to be the greatest
healing power in existence.

<u>fourth wise king</u>

i am the fourth wise king
the one who missed the northern star
got turned around in the desert
unknowing of where you are

lord my head is heavy
this crown too much to hold
but i fear if i take it off
i will not grow old

<u>creator and crafter</u>

we are what we have established ourselves
to be,
and i have often wondered why i chose to be
cold
in the eyes of those who make me feel like
i am burning.

<u>your eyes tell</u>
<u>to say "stay gold"</u>

join me darling in a city of soul; where
you can dance until morning.
heaven's music continuous—
notes lulling your heart. here you can
journey to love yourself and
tomorrow you will awaken
joyous and serendipitous.

<u>periods in paragraphs</u>

and so, we break,
but our breaking points are merely
periods in paragraphs—
brief pauses to catch our breath
and continue on.

<u>be kind</u>

acknowledge the darkness
and coax it to lull into a slumber—
for often times the darkness knows
nothing else but destruction
when it never wanted to be
a creature of chaos at all.

<u>addicted to desire</u>

dreams...
such beautiful, impossible beings,
far more addictive than any drug or action—
for once they are fulfilled
there is always a need
for a higher dosage.

<u>poker or roulette?</u>

a gambler—
that is what we have become—
addicted to the possibility
of a future we wish for.
go ahead, you are at the table now,
throw your chips and roll the dice.

<u>willful ignorance is a crime, you know</u>

one day we will become
wise enough to listen
to the warnings fear speaks.
but until then they will remain
unnoticed, and we will reap
the consequences of our
willful ignorance.

between God and me

"a demon!" preacher cried,
pointing a crooked finger at me—
teeth yellow and gnarled,
head swimming in scriptures.
so i turned around to see hell's creature
but a mirror stared back.
"douse yourself in lies,"
i shouted. "cherry-pick the truth,
but how could you know my heart
when you only spent time
with skeletons and cadavers."

april's flowers

when we find the ability to collect
compassion
like plucking flowers in an overflowing
garden,
then we can see each other as humans
rather than those who are least monster-
like.

~~strike~~

recognizing what is
good and bad for us
is the initial draft
of our story.
whether we choose to edit or not
is the decision that
encourages or inhibits
our greatness.

<u>justify me</u>

if persephone had not been dragged
to the depths of hell perhaps
there would not be beauty in death…
but that thought never stopped
demeter's tears.

incurable

is it not exhausting to be a perfectionist?
to want to be what you cannot,
and though you are destined
to fall ever-so short,
you pry yourself from the ground,
scraping off all the failure
of what you believed yourself not to be,
only to jump from that building again.
eventually, we will realize
that no being can fly naturally
without wings.

<u>oh, what a beautiful flower you would make</u>

a rose is still a weed no matter its color.
if you will it to be a flower
it will do nothing but strangle a garden.
do not tie your own noose
pretending to be what you are not.

<u>beyond the signs that read "stay away"</u>
<u>we play</u>

the things that overwhelm us are
what we cannot control, bursts of
human or inhuman emotion that
make us feel as though
the very vines on trees
have reached out with prickly fingers
to choke us.
recklessly, we decide to cut down the tree
that carries the vine without ever
pondering
whether we should have walked
into that forbidden forest
in the first place.
perhaps we deserved our pain,
venturing where we were warned
not to go.

idol

happiness is an abstract being,
yet we force it all too often
to fit into the presence of a person
then are disappointed when the beauty
of such person
does not match the perfect image
in our minds.

<u>breathe</u>

to feel is the intake of breath
and to heal is the exhale.
so, why are you standing there
turning blue in the face?

<u>uncovering us</u>

will we ever cease to fear
showing who we are
even with those we love?
can we ever truly open up
while knowing there will
always be a door shut—
and behind that door
is who we are
but what we cannot bear
to lose?

<u>oh, hello there?</u>

when we lose ourselves,
where do we go?
it is quite jarring to appear
within ourselves like a ghost
come back to life
when we did not realize
we died in the first place.

<u>to deal with you,</u>
<u>my trauma</u>

i huddled under the blanket,
a book in my hand
and used it to buffer my trauma
shouting, "this is my home,
and though it is not real
it is mine,
and you cannot have it."

<u>the early bird misses the dragonfly</u>

run as if you were flying
on dragonfly wings—
do not listen
as the birds sing.
such sweet siren songs—
such sharp beaks.
yes, fly through the night
while the nightingale sleeps—
though the nightingale
never sleeps at night.

<u>gifting</u>

a book of poetry,
not all particularly good,
but because it was a gift
you accepted and read it—
and although it is no odyssey,
i hope you enjoy it.

<u>down</u>
<u>upside</u>

green skies and blue ground—
it seems we have been turned around.
since when was happiness this consistent?
a breath without the burning constant—
white waves and blue sand.
topsy-turvy land.

irrelevant consistency

rhyme, monkey, rhyme
but even with all the time
to rhyme each day
would serve no purpose
if life itself
is inconsistent.

poison burns

do these poems make sense?
probably not—
my thoughts have turned basic
because to be prolific
you must see the world
in a light other than toxic.

<u>i am here</u>

think of me as a beach
on the boardwalk shore.
lean your weary head
against my shoulder.
i will be here until you
regain your strength.

abused tigers and circus stripes

i spat fire and raged,
tore and shredded,
anyone who came close
to my cage.
because this was a haven—
or so i was told.
but dear mr. stockholm syndrome
these bars make a lousy home.
so, i think i will go.

<u>sadist</u>

i have carried these sins
i know of their weight,
so i promise you there is no need
to press down on this bag
to crack my shoulders
so that i may remember
the mistakes i have made.

<u>the curse of naïveté</u>

how dare you speak
and call me naïve
when you have never known
the horror of being me?

assumptions

i have walked so many lives—
fought my fair share of demons,
so do not think me empty-headed
when i sit somewhere grinning.

<u>a snippet of a conversation</u>

yes, i am, i am ranting,
and i will rant for today.
you see only stilted progress,
but it keeps my demons at bay.

<u>i will not name you</u>
<u>as you are me</u>

never to be titled
for no one is meant to be here
and if you are
this is for you
and only you

<u>how do i say i am lonely?</u>

you do not have to be alone
to be lonely
loneliness is not so simple
it is a crack in the soul
without the right words
to stitch it back together

<u>in lead memories</u>

they crossed me out in black pen,
scribbling lines over my name
because i was so *wrong*
that no one would see me
as anything other than a mistake—
twisted in ways unmeant to be—
unacceptable in my disfigurement.
but a small part remained of me
that they could never erase,
for once lead has struck the page
an imprint will remain.

incompatible

i did not realize how much i dreamt
until you dragged me down to earth
and told me it was right to stay grounded.
but now i pity you for believing only
what your eyes can gossip about,
for you lay with ignorance
in your thoughts
when you believe them to be useless.

<u>books to wash me away</u>

it seems my only mistake
was living so many lives
that i forgot to live mine
and left my name behind.

<u>cruel teacher</u>

"sometimes you must learn
how to swim by drowning,"
you said hurling me into the sea,
and i drowned just like you said.
but you did not tell me
it would be so dark at the depths
that i would not be able to see.
so, how can you blame me
when i got turned around
and swam down and down and down?

<u>a prayer</u>

lord help me
for i have not seen the sun
rise today

<u>a muffled voice of a ghost's past</u>

her silence was the loudest
i had ever heard,
and it shook the world
in such a way
that it never changed.

strange jealousy

i envy the pencil shavings
for i wish to be brushed aside
and forgotten about
to have people turn their eyes
and disregard my existence
so that i may have a moment
of peace laying on the floor

soulmates in equality

i never wanted a hero
just someone to lean on
and who can lean on me
to find my other half
as strong and weak as i

to heal a broken heart

my heart bled,
and bled, and bled, and bled,
and bled, and bled, and bled,
to rebuild and heal.

<u>a future of none</u>

the cards dealt have no face
blank tarot cards and empty spells
and the glass ball fills with no fog
and the fortune teller weeps

<u>snow</u>

and i realized that we were like snow—
we fell, melted, and dissolved
before we let go.

can coal be returned?

i do not know why i cry on christmas—
the happiest day of the year,
but it must have something to do
with you not being here.

<u>a promise for a thousand mornings
or perhaps more</u>

he asked me what i would do
when his light would fade away,
and i told him i would sit with him
until nighttime dawned to day.

<u>cruel teacher ii</u>

they said i was swimming—
swimming in dangerous waters,
and i laughed and cried,
"of course, it is only natural to learn
after you have drowned for years."

<u>echoes of anamnesis</u>
<u>ode to lost eulogies</u>

who shall the forgotten be?
years have passed, i dare to say,
there is no one left to remember me.

and though no mortal had a guess,
and all memory soon betrays,
who shall the forgotten be?

an enigma to all, i must confess,
it seems they have sealed the gateway.
there is no one left to remember me.

we drip of predestined distress.
still, we wail and weep from far away,
who shall the forgotten be?

our nuances begin to coalesce,
only He can make our spirits unmade.
there is no one left to remember me.

and so, my memory will regress—
and so, to earth my body decay—
who shall the forgotten be?
there is no one left to remember me.

<u>to my miscarried sibling</u>

my life has continued on without you.
i do not remember when my mother
carried you during the pregnancy,
but even so, you have pressed yourself
into our existence—
not through endless grief,
but in the time stamped between
my younger brother and me,
and that time, my unborn sibling,
is only yours to claim.

<u>gpa or sat</u>

how awful i have found
numbers to be
when it was their sole purpose
to define me.

<u>a moment in solidarity for death's</u>
<u>confusion</u>

death is surely in for a surprise,
for i can only imagine its shock
when it intends to grip my heart,
injecting winter into red veins,
but comes and finds it already frozen—
oh, what a poor ancient being.

set sail on a sunny day

on the edge of a ship
i looked over the edge
wrapping-paper water
that is endlessly wrinkled
and i look down
at the shimmering
and i wonder about the depth
but how am i supposed
to find an answer of how deep
when i have not seen the bottom
to my own trauma yet

true power

your words wielded correctly
could command armies,
bring down nations,
destroy and rebuild
better and new. . .
but none of that
can be accomplished
if you are not healthy too.

<u>demonetized</u>

no, i do not struggle
with mental illness.
actually, my grades
are quite high
in that class.
i am very good
at being fucked up
in the head.
oh, to struggle—
how lovely.

imaginary gatekeeper

"bring me to the keeper
of futures and class,"
and you will not be able
to answer what i asked
because no true barrier
forms an impenetrable wall
between who you are now
and someone who can change the world.

<u>sunfish</u>

no one captures my heart
quite like a musician
who draws feelings from notes
while i put them into words.
they are the push and i the pull
on this wave of emotional sailing.
rock me to a peaceful rest,
my musician, or give me the sails,
for i was once quite good
at manning a sunfish.

rebellion knows intelligence well

they love us ignorant—
laugh at us bumbling buffoons
because if we fight one another
we will not bother to wonder who
pinned us against each other.

<u>models and beauty queens</u>
<u>made into monsters</u>

straighten your teeth,
brush out your hair,
and yet still you are not
beautiful anywhere.
society is a beast
that is never full
but you, my dear,
have fed it well.

<u>winter evenings</u>

bundled beneath a quilted blanket,
i sipped on lavender tea.
to be warm when it was snowing
i knew was a luxury—
one i was quick to indulge in,
soaking in the warmth
to sear out the sadness.

back to basics

my sword has grown heavy.
it is spotted with bloodstains,
and i do not think i can
lift it again,
and i cannot imagine another battle.
but the first lesson taught
is to pick up your heavy boots.
so, i lifted my legs again,
and again, and again.

<u>lost in an ancient forest</u>

the words whisper to me
on a silver breeze,
gently caressing and rustling
the emerald trees.
"be kind... be at peace.
live, and breathe, and be."

<u>the sick do not know the difference</u>

the windowsill sounds like a siren's song
so beautiful, alluring, and old
and yet, those who jump never knew
the dangers that unfolded
when they swam into the rocks,
half-dead, and were eaten half-alive.

<u>blackthorne: the border</u>

i have never been to my homeland
but it resonates in my heart
so i take a shaky breath
and off-pitch start
and i sing of lonely shadows
and i sing of a cold world
and i sing of a game
that is divide and rule
and i sing of changing pathways
for the children's lives at stake
and i sing of tolerance and equality
and i sing of forgiving past mistakes
and i sing of difficulty
and the price of living free
and to make a border
my grandmother never knew
into a memory

<u>heed the jester's jokes</u>

welcome to a courtly party
please allow me to serve you
with a great jester's story
a cold queen atop a throne of steel
and she is commanding and cruel
dictating even her soldier's wounds to heal
lick them like dogs, sheep to slaughter
and no matter the truth of it all
you will still fill this queen's hall
with laughter

<u>forgotten gods</u>

boulders piled atop each other
made by gods of forgotten religions
as the stars who could recall their names
shine and remain mute
mystery
the night loves mystery

mountain command

"climb," the gravel mountain commanded,
but there was no foothold to catch a sole,
the piling mistakes rendering you
as helpless as icarus, falling and burning.

the dark lord ruling blood river

treason, treason—
i will pull apart my thoughts,
betray the demons ruled by a dark lord
who used to be the childhood me.
but i will face her in a river that runs of
blood.
i was no ajax— no achillies—
no, ares would never favor a traitor.
but as i stared at myself,
i gritted my teeth,
and decided that i was not echo either,
and i refused to be forgotten.

<u>you were always enough</u>

do not fear the outskirts, dear,
venture outside the pre-drawn lines.
we are not prepackaged minions.
conformity is where creativity dies.

coffee shop book lady

she had a smattering of freckles with a
tall frame,
and a carefully placed smile in her
twenties.
her hazel eyes crinkled when she spoke,
and her brown-coppery locks swayed when she
nodded.
a book well-worn clutched between her
fingers,
and gentle dark circles under her eyes.
she drank enough coffee to kill a man,
but the world did not know her name.

<u>snake woods</u>

there was a creek that we skipped
or fell into dependent on the day
an open forest and snake woods
where we would chase each other and play
for hours we mapped that forest
avoiding copperheads and chasing deer
getting pricked by the prickle bushes
and climbing that one japanese maple
then once done exploring we would lean over
sticky with sweat and
check each other for ticks
hasty creatures in a world of monsters
but we thought we ruled all of it

omens of hellfire

how do we fight against
what we cannot see,
beyond the realm of
our perceived realities
that interlaced into our futures
like omens of hellfire?

<u>highway</u>

the signs are invisible
on the highway
so we drive up mountains
cross bridges and boulders
but it is an enigma as to
our destination
still we drive unknowing
where we are supposed to be
and we drive unknowing
what awaits us at the exit

<u>obsessive observers</u>

pity the poppies
those beautiful petals
only worn by mourners
only mentioned at funerals

<u>i never liked spiders</u>

i never liked spiders
i do not know why
maybe those spidery legs
have touched me too many times
but what i feel towards them
i feel towards some people
when i am not sure their intentions
i treat each one as lethal

<u>back to our roots</u>

"bake me a cake
as fast as you can,"
she echoes in a dark room
to expel that feeling of that man.

truth hurts

when you said that
i felt like i skinned my knees
when the flesh broke open
and i began to bleed
you then came around
with the neosporin i needed
but i shoved it away
gritting my teeth
because you added pain to my injury
while doing what was best for me

<u>a thing with. . .</u>
<u>what did emily say?</u>

white wings,
black beak,
a promised future
is all i need.

un-sutchered wounds

i will never forget that day.
from a lofted pickup truck
a man shouted slurs at you—
horrid, awful words for just existing,
and you looked back at me,
smiled, and shrugged,
then came to give me a hug
as i sobbed in your arms
over your daily recurrence.

<u>it builds</u>

bruises in the shape of hands—
on her wrists— on her breasts.
five stitches to sew her back up,
so she would not bleed on the sheets.
torn muscles and choke marks,
but her eyes— her eyes were empty
because he took her life, did he not?
now, out in the streets her sister cries,
"death penalty to all men
who think they are entitled to our skin.
their punishment should not be
a rape penalty.
it should be murder—
murder in the first degree."

tally my days

"your days are numbered,"
they whispered from the dark,
but i grinned at my shadows,
moon-white teeth sharp as broken bone,
a flash of a knife in the night.
"my days were numbered
upon my first breath,
and it is those pesky invisible numbers
that will lead to my death."

the remnants

the chains are broken,
shackles shattered in shards,
and there is a crack in the ceiling
that lets in the world,
and there i sat for a decade,
perhaps even more,
chained to the floor.
only once I returned to the cell
in my head— in my heart—
and my first thought upon entry was,
"it is quite cold and dark
the stone here is too damp for a hearth
perhaps i will go home."

<u>willow whispers</u>

"it is a cycle
it is a cycle
it is a cycle,"
the willow whispers.
"pain will fade,
happiness will begin,
and we will start again
on a new cycle."

the first dawn without me

when the first dawn comes without me
and i do not wake from sleep,
i hope you close your eyes tight
and do not think of me.

the waves will break upon the sand
and rain splatter on the pavement,
but from where i took up space in your life
there will be no movement.

i slept and drifted off,
for it was time for me.
all of us have calling cards
for when it is time to leave.

winter will still melt to spring
when the sun has left my eyes,
and in my most cherished wishes
i hope you continue with your life.

the dawn will be beautiful
right after i pass away,
and i am sorry i am not there
to wipe your tears that day.

the prism of color will shine
especially bright for you,
so that you may know while you miss me
that i also miss you too.

<u>growing roots</u>

he shook his head,
pointing one damning finger
toward the wet soil
and said, "here,
i will plant my roots
to face my trauma."
but time did not bother
to spare him a glance
and continued onward.

<u>questioning</u>

writing is isolating,
a private affair—
but it is lonely
inside my head,
and every time i write
it is so that
i am not lonely.
so, where does that
leave me?

<u>carnivorous dogs</u>

it is not a pretty image—
to see the living dead—
the home where
the carnivorous dogs
are fed... there,
inside my head.

for protection i will create a monster

this part of me is guarded
for there is a demon at the door
afraid that if you look too closely
you will risk taking what it hoards

pillow forts instead of pinot noir

too much alcohol swimming
in my heart— in my head
and i am far too tired to sleep
and fall into my own bed
so i will build a tower of pillows
and try to become a child again
when i did not drink but dreamed instead

house hunting

i want windows,
glass pane from floor to ceiling.
let there be light
to grace the space.
yes, windows to let in the light—
light that lets darkness sleep.

petals or rainwater

do not be the petals in my life,
beautiful, but quickly plucked by the
breeze.
be my stem reaching up to the sky
or be the rain to water me.
your presence in my life might add to
appearance,
but what good is popularity without a
heart?

sticks and stones

words do not sting,
they bury,
grave diggers with shovels,
like a parasite beneath skin.
they do not fade like a slap—
there, sting, gone,
they devour— they feast.

<u>perhaps this is unoriginal</u>

it is time you arise
open your eyes
and recognize
that this is your life
and no one will live it
but you

pointillism

i want to be dot art
because i have never felt connected,
and my being makes up an image
that i cannot make sense of.

<u>the clowns and the insane</u>

a person labeled a clown
will always be a joke
just as a person labeled insane
will never be a rational thinker
so we can laugh when a clown cries
and label our dissenters as crazy
to control them

but if the insane demanded voices
and the clowns wiped off their smiles
those who would be worried
are of high society
for how can they control those
who no longer allow themselves
to be labeled

<u>someone once told me</u>

you cower behind words,
masquerading as an escape—
to avoid your daily problems—
to take up the least amount of space.

<u>history's writers</u>

have you forgotten your stories
are re-read, re-written, and edited,
put into a show,
reliant on the pertinent fact
that the dead cannot correct you?

<u>encouraging abuse</u>

sing me a song, my muse.
louder! you can sing better!
so beautiful, you used to be.
what happened? you can do better. . .
you can be better.
you used to be better.
what happened?

time traveler's revelation

i went back to the past
where my memories began,
and i found just that. . .
memories.
there is no future in the past
only old melodies
that are only sweet forgotten
and would not sound nearly as beautiful
when replayed tomorrow morning.

popop, our country failed you

he fought and bled for our country,
watched his friends die horrific deaths
in a war he was set to draft into,
and said he felt the most unsafe
on american soil,
because he did not bleed in vietnam
more than he did wearing his uniform
in boston.

stalker

trauma followed behind you,
close enough to smell the decay
of seared and dead yesterdays.
it sung loudly when you spoke
then turned into a ghost
when anyone looked its way.
you spent so much time annoyed,
trying to ignore its screaming laugh,
that you never looked forward
into the future,
far too concerned with looking back.

grilled cheese and autumn leaves

pumpkins sat perched on the pavement,
red and orange leaves
twirling to the ground,
unmoored sky dancers floating gently down,
the sunset amplifying their colors,
mirroring it on a large screen
stretching far past the horizon.
as i take cover from the chilling wind
behind a large oak tree trunk,
i cannot help but wonder why it is
that i still cut my sandwiches diagonal
into two little triangles
like my mother used to.

floating in the cosmos

humans live on a floating rock
circling the sun in space,
our jobs and lives minimal at best,
for our earth will rotate without us—
our species a mere blink in time.
but we find ways to give life meaning—
to give us meaning,
and if our meaning is determined by us
why are we letting fear control us
it is quite pointless. . .
is it not?

<u>placing down the pen</u>

there is a death that every writer
experiences
where they sit in front of paper,
pen perched,
and wonder, "will my writings be read when
i am gone?"
and because their writings cannot answer
the question
they place down their pen and leave the
paper blank.

a note from the epicenter

we are quarantined like plagued rats—
forced into our homes and refused air.
it seems all of america has turned into a
jail.
i have heard many times,
"you are lucky you live alone."
but i would rather be exposed to an
exposure
than spend another minute listening through
my walls.
the only time i hear a human voice is when
it is screamed,
muffled by the plaster, spoken in another
set of lives.
i clean repeatedly because that is all that
is left.
i have read all the books on my shelves,
and in the stifling silence
i have forgotten how my parents call my
name.
months in solitude, a solitary confinement
for protection,
and many-a-times i have thought of leaving
in the hopes that my breathless death
may have some noise.

march 20, 2020

toilet paper is gone from the shelves.
now metal is the only choice for bread.
the virus has not reached us and yet,
we act as though we are the epicenter.
and so, the race begins,
not to outrun the virus,
but to outlive each other.

<u>the old politician</u>

he sat in the capital building
clicking his pen through another bill.
the voting would happen— the bill would
fail
all decided prior to the introduction of
it.
he looked down at the paper before him—
what he had scribbled on the page
and, for a moment, hopelessness set in
when he read his subconscious thoughts,
"sometimes good people get punished
for doing the right things."

<u>battery of me</u>

battered wife syndrome,
and the sheets within my hands,
years of repeated abuse
by myself— within my house.

tics

he did not use to tic,
but he did after he got jumped.
the world decided life was
too perfect— too peaceful for him,
so it filled his life with the
incessant need to move.

questions to my crim teacher

what does it mean to be 'reasonable'
when none of us are?
so how can that be the standard
of the correct way to handle behavior
when we all act irrational in fear?

i understand

i understand
i wish i did not but i do
just like how i know each spring will fade
until i have seen my last
and i will not know which it is—
will not know when to say
all i fail to speak now

i understand
i know why you left
but that does not mean i cannot
feel your absence beside me
and what i do not understand—
do not know— cannot comprehend
is why it lingers for so long

<u>discussing remedies</u>

"drink chamomile tea.
it will make you feel better."
"but i only have green tea."
"well, green tea does not work
so that is a bust."
"should i drink green tea?"
"no. you need chamomile. go buy chamomile."
"i cannot. i have no money."
"but you need chamomile tea."
"but i cannot afford it."

media coverage

we take the mic from truth
to give it to ease
because truth was never easy
to listen to,
but now the louder it shouts
the less we hear
because its teachings are not
reaching our ears.

<u>kids that we were</u>

as children we knew no monsters,
attune to acute pain and no more,
innocence and excitement in dope dosages.
when we fell, we scraped our palms and bled
then dusted off our pants to try the trick
again.
we ignored the wound because it would mend
that knowledge of getting better—
never questioning our friends' loyalty
because pain did not linger. . . it faded,
and the worst portion was the initial
instance
not the continuation on—

<u>sitting on a deck with my thoughts</u>

my doubts began a game—
those ones that i have to overcome—
a quick round of russian roulette,
but there is always a bullet
in my chamber of the gun.

a last flight

do not cry darling
you cannot reverse the tides
an earthquake will shake the ground
    no matter how you try to quell it
somethings in this life will happen
    no matter how you try to stronghold it
for every pilot has their last flight
so keep your eyes toward the horizon
    and enjoy the feeling of flying

change the rape laws

i stood in a ring facing an opponent—
two times my size, two times my weight—
and i braced myself to fight as he charged.
then hands landed on my arms,
holding me in place so i could not move
as the first of many punches rained down.
through my bloody and swollen face,
i turned to you, my love, and said,
"help me."
but you held me down as i was battered
and replied, "but what if i get hurt?"
worried over a possibility instead of
reality.
so, i bled out in the ring as you watched
and whispered delicately in my ear,
"if you are losing then fight harder."

<u>only the rich cry</u>

i am rich— wealth in my hands
coffers filled with tears
the currency of pain
because those who are poor
have no time to spare— to mourn

<u>seasons pass</u>

"you will understand when you are older."
okay.
but i still do not understand. . .
and i am beginning to realize
that you never had an answer.

suspended

you grew bored
of the perpetual falling,
never quite hitting the ground
the only sound the rush of air—
and, of course, you were lonely there,
so you kept falling through darkness,
spinning through days in a daze,
and cynically you hoped to
land or hit the ground,
either one to stop the falling.
repetition was quite mundane.

homeless and wandering

am i less human without a home
wandering about the world without an anchor
no place to rest— to claim of "from"
just "here and there and everywhere"
i wonder if a sailboat loses its purpose
when its lone sailor decides to desert it
will they both lose identities being apart
sometimes beneath the stars i hope
that my home is lonely without me

sunshine after hours

it is a good life
just a bad day,
and sometimes you have to
think of it that way.

<u>a closing</u>

all good things come to a close,
or perhaps this will just be a chapter
of a very long and healthy book
where we grow together
and learn how to get back
to who we once were before we were broken.
sleep well and dream through your days.
may your pathways make you wander,
may your adventures never fade—
and one day
somewhere in the spring or fall
i will sit beside you and say,
"look at you... you made it."

Made in the USA
Coppell, TX
04 April 2022

75991078R00100